5 GOLDEN KEYS TO YOUR LIFE PURPOSE

Discover Your Master Key to Really Living

MARCELENE ANDERSON

5 GOLDEN KEYS TO YOUR LIFE PURPOSE
DISCOVER YOUR MASTER KEY TO REALLY LIVING

iUniverse books may be ordered through booksellers or by contacting:

iUniverse
1663 Liberty Drive
Bloomington, IN 47403
www.iuniverse.com
844-349-9409

ISBN: 978-1-6632-2909-0 (sc)
ISBN: 978-1-6632-2910-6 (e)

Library of Congress Control Number: 2021919326

Print information available on the last page.

iUniverse rev. date: 11/02/2021

Contents

Book Contents vii

Preface xi

Chapter 1   Introduction 1

    Exercise: What Is My Purpose? 4

    The Purpose Self-Assessment 11

PART 1
Unlocking Your Life Purpose

Chapter 2   Golden Key #1: People 15

    Key 1: People 15

    Life decisions I made about who I want to be 19

    Behaviors are values in Action 21

    Further Reflections 24

Chapter 3   Golden Key #2: Pain 26

    Key 2: Pain 26

    Transforming Your Pain 26

Chapter 4   Golden Key #3: Proven Skills 36

    Key 3: Proven Skills 36

    Identifying Your Skills and Abilities 40

    Integrating Talents and Abilities with Your Life Purpose 46

Chapter 5   Golden Key #4: Passion 49

    Key 4: Passion 49

    Know What Brings You Joy and Satisfaction 52

Chapter 6   Golden Key #5: Putting It Together 53

    Key 5: Putting It Together 53

Put it All Together: Your Master Key, Your Life-Purpose..... 54

Life-Purpose Checklist.. 55

PART 2

Living Your Purpose

Chapter 7   Choosing Empowering Beliefs.......................... 59

Believe In Yourself 62

Chapter 8   Using Failure as A Stepping Stone 67

Dealing with Failure... 70

Chapter 9   Accelerate Living Your Life-Purpose 74

Warning: Don't Expect this Great Journey to be Easy 76

Epilogue... 81

Purpose Quiz Answers.. 83

Examples of Life Purpose.. 84

References 87

About The Author... 89

Further Study To Discover Your Life Purpose 93

About the Author... 97

Book Contents

Preface

1. Introduction – The 5 Keys To Unlocking Your Life Purpose

PART 1 – Discovering Your Life Purpose

2. Key 1: People – Choosing Who You Want to Be
3. Key 2: Pain – Transforming Pain, Turning Scars into Stars
4. Key 3: Proven Skills & Abilities – Using Your Skills & Abilities to Make a Difference
5. Key 4: Passion – Living with Passion
6. Key 5: Putting It All Together – Creating Your Purpose Master Key

PART 2 – Living Your Purpose

7. Choosing Empowering Beliefs
8. Using Failure as a Stepping Stone
9. Accelerating the Living of Your Purpose

Answer Key: What is My Purpose Quiz
Examples: Purpose Statement

References
About the Author
Other Books by the Author
Getting In Touch with the Author
Further Study to Discover Your Life Purpose

I have written this guide to realize my life purpose, to
help others discover and live their purpose, to
satisfy their heart-and-soul's calling.

I am deeply grateful to countless numbers of persons
who have provided lessons for me on my life journey,
helping me to answer the 5 key questions
to discover and increasingly realize
my life purposes.

I am especially grateful for friends, Susan Anderson,
for initial editing of my manuscript and to
Dain Supero for his superb final editing,
elevating it to a masterpiece.

Preface

"Find your own path and tread it with absolute faith and confidence.
It is foolishness to try and walk in someone else's footsteps and try
to imitate them in what they are doing. Until you know your own
special path you will try one path after another – seeking, seeking,
always seeking; but when you eventually find your path nothing and
no one will be able to turn you from it, and that path will carry
you to the ultimate goal: Your realization of oneness with me."
- Eillen Caddy, Footsteps on the Path

You may be wondering, 'what is this oneness?' It is your inner calling.

I believe each of us enters life with a purpose. Regrettably, most of us leave without ever accomplishing it. Many leave this world realizing they had their sights set on all the wrong things. Some leave without ever having set their sights. It evokes the song lyrics, "Is this, all there is?"

Why are you here? What is your purpose? These are questions worth our time. Unfortunately, we can't Google our unique life purpose, at least not yet. Perhaps one day the internet will answer these questions, but would that not take the joy out of discovering for ourselves? Would that not erase the journey that we must create for ourselves?

1- Songwriter David Hidalgo / Louis Frausto Perez, From the Album By the Light of the Moon, Singer Los Lobos

The tried, tested, and true way to find the answers is to ask the right questions, to take organized action, and to seek the answers within. Even if you don't yet understand your life purpose, know that you were born with one. We all have our calling, waiting to be heard. This is your opportunity and, in a way, your responsibility to discover that unique purpose.

Identifying, clarifying, confirming, affirming, and honoring your life-purpose is the most important and fulfilling endeavour you will undertake regardless of your professional endeavours. This realization is a fundamental belief common to all successful people. It is the undeniable path to their success.

Over the years I have asked myself some core questions about who I am. I have soul-searched, asking what is God, and what I should do with my life. At an Individual and Family workshop I attended, we were asked to explore our life purpose. At the end of my life, I was asked, what would I want people to say about me? How would I want to be remembered, and what would I want on my tombstone? I can recall, at that moment, considering the kind of person I wanted to be and what my life purpose was about.

I am fortunate to have faced these questions. Within them I found the chance to reflect and discover myself. My own life purpose, it turns out, is *to be a loving person who helps others know and realize their purpose.*

I have expressed my life purpose in a number of service roles over the years. My work has involved helping individuals and organizations find their purpose, their vision for the future, and the results that they want to achieve. I have done this by planning, developing, and implementing strategies for personal and organizational self-discovery.

Many years ago, I worked at an organization where I developed corporate training programs for employees, which I found quite meaningful. A re-organization of the department, however, divided us into separate units. I along with two colleagues were assigned to a new unit, where we no longer found our roles to be meaningful. We used an old assembly line analogy to describe our jobs: we felt as if we worked in a toaster factory, where we made an element for the toasters, but did not know what a toaster was. We felt disconnected from the big picture, our organization's larger purpose. Research indicates that only 30–40% of employees are meaningfully engaged in their work. Many primarily work for a paycheck and dream of winning the lottery so that they can do something they love. Purpose, the inner spark that gives life meaning and fulfilment, is missing for them.

Individual purpose and organizational purpose are essential to each other. The greater the convergence between them, the greater the individual's confidence in knowing that they are in the right place. For them, work is no longer just a means to earn a paycheck. It's a means to a purpose. See figure 1, below.

Figure 1: Employee and Organizational Purpose Alignment

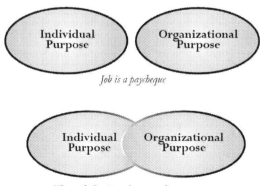

Job is a paycheque

The workplace is a place to realize my purpose.

The stronger the alignment between individual and organizational purpose, the stronger the sense of belonging and compatibility for employees. It feels like being at the right place, working together to achieve something significant. This synergy takes both individual and organization to realize. Organizations do not, and cannot, hand you your life purpose. Only you can discover and claim it.

Clarifying your purpose in a written statement anchors you. It becomes your cornerstone for building a meaningful life. Upon discovering your purpose, you can take action that will take you where you are meant to go. You can find or create an organization with the capacity to turn your vision into reality.

CHAPTER 1

Introduction
5 Golden Keys to Your Life Purpose

People have and give many reasons why they are not successful. You may have heard some of these reasons, and you have probably used some of them yourself:

- I don't have enough education.
- I don't have the right connections.
- I didn't graduate from high school, college, university or any other academic institution.
- I have to make a living and can't risk that pursuing my so-called purpose.
- I'm not old enough, young enough, smart enough, tall enough, short enough, rich enough. It's usually "not something enough."
- Otherwise, it's "if only." If only I had this resource, then I would be successful.

Is that truly the reason why countless individuals are not successful? According to success coach Richard Leider, the number one reason why people fail is not for lack of education or the right connections, or any of the reasons listed above.

The #1 reason people fail is that they do not have a clear purpose.

They are like airplanes departing for nowhere, destination unknown, spending decades circling around.

It's not difficult to spot the symptoms of a life without clear purpose. Without a definite basis for being here and for doing what they do, individuals:

- Feel unfulfilled, as though they are sleepwalking through their lives
- Fill their lives with hours of unfruitful activities like gossiping, television, and social media
- Engage in addictions of many forms: shopping, complaining, sports, alcohol, drugs, and even work
- Suffer from depression and, worst of all, are more prone to suicide

I once lived in a growing affluent suburb of Seattle, where I met the mortician who served the area. He recounted a shocking story about how most of his funerals were for homemakers who committed suicide. These women and their families had sought the good life in this idealistic community, but they instead found themselves isolated and stranded in suburbia. They had limited connection with others and many lacked a definite and clear purpose apart from their families, regardless of how much they loved them. It just wasn't enough to make them wake up wanting to do something significant.

Many native communities have a higher rate of suicide than the general population, particularly youth suicides. When they, like the housemakers of some utopian neighbourhood, cannot see hope or a compelling purpose for their lives, they also tend to end their lives prematurely.

In his book *Man's Search for Meaning*, Viktor Frankl writes that in the Nazi concentration camp where he was imprisoned, prisoners who lost their purpose and their faith in the future died a few days after giving up. Instead of losing purpose, Frankl would often quote German philosopher Nietzsche, who once said, "He that has a *why* to live can bear with almost any *how*."

As a prisoner, Frankl envisioned himself giving a lecture at Carnegie Hall in New York, which gave him the purpose that kept him alive. Frankl knew, and saw, that without a vision for their lives, his fellow prisoners would all perish. Without something to live for, how can anyone endure struggle?

The ancient wisdom of Proverbs 13 reminds us, "Without a vision, people perish."

Without purpose, people soon perish. I would go so far as to say that without purpose, people never really live.

Purpose Defined

George Bernard Shaw says we are at our best when we know where we are going and why, and when we operate from a clear sense of purpose. This sense of purpose has been described in many ways:

a. Destiny
b. A Life Path
c. A Sacred Contract
d. A Unique Calling

Which of these descriptions best captures your life purpose?

Benefits of "Discovering" Your Purpose

The number one cause of failure is lack of definite purpose. When you know your life purpose and when your lifestyle is aligned with it, you:

- Are eager to wake up and start your morning
- Feel centred and grounded
- Value yourself and have good self-esteem
- Reinforce relationships
- Feel like you are using your abilities
- Engage in meaningful activities and work in sync with your purpose
- Live in the present and not the past
- Plan for the future but live for today
- Feel like you are making a difference
- Experience inner-peace

Exercise: What Is My Purpose?

Match the name of each person below with their purpose.

1. Terry Fox

a. Showed mercy and compassion to the dying

2. Mother Theresa

b. Raised money in the fight against cancer

3. President John F. Kennedy

c. Built a device for communicating long distances

4. Charles Lindberg

d. Ended Apartheid

5. Marie Curie

e. Put a man on the moon

6. Alexander Graham Bell

f. Achieved equality for all people

7. Martin Luther King	g. Discovered radium
8. Nelson Mandela	h. First person to fly across the Atlantic Ocean
9. Rosa Parks	i. Freed the Indian people from British rule through nonviolent resistance
10. Mahatma Gandhi	j. Civil rights leader – refused giving up her seat for a white man and moving to the back of the bus

Check your answers with the answer key at the end of the book, page 83.

You may be wondering, "how did these people find their life purpose?" Keep in mind that none of them knew their life purpose when they were born. During the course of their lives, by seeing what was needed, by following their passion and applying their knowledge, they first discovered themselves and then their life purpose.

This book contains the 5 Golden Keys to unlocking your life purpose. In the chapters ahead, you will:

- Identify what you deeply care about
- Transform personal and social pain to help others
- Claim your talents to make a difference in what you do
- Own your passion by embodying your calling in life
- Master your purpose through self-belief and positive action

8 Myths About Purpose You Should Know

Having a purpose makes you feel that you are living your life fully. There are 8 common myths that prevent people from discovering and pursuing their life purpose:

1) I'm not important enough to have a purpose

Some years ago, I received a beautiful card that said, 'Every creature's story is unique with certain truths to tell.' Every bird, every animal, every fish, every plant has its uniqueness. We readily recognize that each has a part to play in the world, a distinct nature, a life purpose. Each is here for a reason.

What about us? Why are we here?

Who are we to say that we are above purpose? Who are we to decide that we are not important enough to claim our uniqueness and our calling in life?

The Creator of the Universe did not make a mistake when you were born.

2) My job is my purpose

It is tempting and convenient to confuse your job with your life purpose. Movies, television, and social media often persuade us into accepting social norms about our purpose, ideas that we accept because they are widely accepted by society. They also blur the line between our core purpose and financial job satisfaction.

Consider jobs you have already had. You may have had the title and the salary, but still couldn't wake up with a smile, ready to take on the world, much less the day. You may have had the opportunity to exercise your purpose, but upon leaving your job you noticed that your purpose was not tied to, or because of, your job.

In some roles you may have experienced great fulfilment, as though you were embodying your life purpose even if you didn't consciously know it at the time. Just remember--you were embodying your purpose. Your job wasn't doing that for you.

3) My life role is my life purpose

It is likewise easy to confuse your life role as your life purpose. You have likely had many roles in life: daughter or son, brother or sister, granddaughter or grandson, nephew or niece, student or teacher, wife or husband, father or mother, employee or employer, friend or rival, board member, shareholder, volunteer, citizen, etc.

Time changes many of these roles. Parents, grandparents, aunts, and uncles pass away. Brothers and sisters get their own lives, frequently in far off places we scarcely visit. Institutionalized education is short-term, even for students who remain campus-bound for post-graduate studies. Marriages at times crumble and partners move on. Children grow up, create and re-create their worlds, become independent and sail with the winds of destiny. Friends come into our lives, some for decades, others briefly. These roles bring joy and satisfaction as they happen, pain and regret when they depart.

I, for instance, am a mother who loves her son dearly. I also have responsibilities as a grandmother. As joyous and memorable as these roles are, they are not my life purpose. Humbly knowing that and honoring each role for its rightful place has given me additional clarity about my life purpose.

4) My purpose has to be grand or help a lot of people

You might think that having a life purpose means you need to change the world as did Mother Theresa, Mahatma Gandhi, or Nelson Mandela. We all know who they became over time, but not who they were when they began—when, as human beings, they likely faced the same fears you now do. Still, you may compare yourself to them and feel you cannot match up. You forget, however, that all they did was repeatedly express their point of view without giving up. They took an unflinching stand for something they cared about deeply. As long as you care about your purpose, as long as you stand for it, it's as grand a purpose as you will find.

5) A purpose must be full of sacrifice or suffering

The idea that you must surrender everything to live your life purpose is among the scariest myths. Although some of us do give up everything and find joy in doing so, many of us fare better in the middle-lane. The idea isn't to have everything; the exact opposite is true. Purpose-driven individuals feel that they pursue, and have, what matters most. Bill Gates, for example, embodied his purpose of using technology to create an easier, more efficient life for individuals and organizations. While realizing his life purpose, he built a highly successful business and became one of the richest men in the world. Today, his wife and he share a passion for using their wealth for philanthropic work. They have evolved their life purpose to tackle severe societal issues such as extreme poverty, poor health, and inadequate education in vulnerable communities around the world.

Another example is Jack Canfield, known for writing Chicken Soup for the Soul. Canfield has sold more books than any other author. His purpose, in the spirit of love and joy, is to inspire people into living their highest vision. He does this by collecting and sharing motivational stories through the Chicken Soup series and his speeches.

As a volunteer at the world-famous Royal Ontario Museum in Toronto, I guided visitors on tours about the adjacent neighbourhood. On one such stroll, I learned about how the wealthy were able to make significant contributions to society, for instance, by bequeathing buildings and by making financial donations.

Perhaps some choose to give up their possessions to follow a life of service to others. That is a truly noble cause, one that should be honoured by those who do not take it upon themselves. But it is not a mandatory cause for everyone. You can start making a big difference with small steps, starting right where you are.

6) I have to change my whole life

A similar myth is that we have to alter our life-paths, give up our families, leave our jobs, become different persons entirely. This, like the previous myth, is fear-based thinking that scares us into playing small, stands between us and bold action. When we live our purpose, we are fully alive, entirely ourselves, and this causes others to gravitate toward us. Some call this 'good energy.'

7) I need to make a living

Sometimes you might think life is an either-or choice, this-or-that game: paying the bills via any job or means available, or doing something that satisfies your spirit. You might try to convince yourself that you can't make a living doing what you love. You scare yourself away from your life purpose. The first step to overcoming this myth is to consider how you can make a living doing what you love.

8) My purpose is just being happy

Another way to live below your full potential is by thinking that satisfaction and fulfillment amount to happiness. Such thinkers drift along doing what they have always been doing, seeking momentary fill-ups of their feel-good gas tanks. They remain stuck in the hamster wheel, always going without getting anywhere, not knowing where or why they're going. They misperceive reality.

> *"Many people have the wrong idea of what constitutes true happiness.*
> *Through fidelity to a worthy purpose, you attain happiness."*
> - Helen Keller, US blind & deaf educator (1880 – 1968)

Purpose as a Process

Finding your life purpose is a process of self-discovery. The treasure you seek is within you, the clues within in your mind, heart, and soul. They have both always been there, but you may not yet have recognized the clues.

Antique dealers sometimes visit homes to identify and appraise objects of value. My late father-in-law was an avid antique collector. He once spotted a table on an outdoor porch and asked the owner if she would be willing to sell it to him. She replied saying she didn't know why he would want the table; she used it only for ironing her curtains. But my father-in-law had a good-eye for antiques. He also knew how to restore them. He saw what the woman could not, the table's potential. This book will help you see your purpose more clearly.

A farmer in Africa brought home a large rock, which he used as a doorstop. One day a stranger recognized it as much more than just an ordinary rock. Inside this doorstop was one of the most valuable gems in the world, the Star Sapphire. We are all like that rock in a way, because within us all lives great potential, waiting to be discovered.

The Golden Keys will help you discover your unique calling, unlock your potential, and heighten your clarity surrounding your life purpose.

A colleague of mine recently had a breakthrough insight about his purpose. With this breakthrough came clarity, self-belief, and a path he could follow. Prior to that, he had not consciously claimed his life purpose. He had no definite path to walk.

Getting clarity about life purpose provides tremendous relief, a sense of inner peace, and genuine satisfaction. It feels like your inner compass is finally working.

The Purpose Self-Assessment

Rate your life purpose on a scale of 1 – 4:

1 – Strongly Disagree	2 – Somewhat Disagree	3 – Somewhat Agree	4 – Strongly Agree

1. I wake up energized most mornings, eager to start the day.
2. I am passionate about my work and my role in life.
3. I know my talents and abilities, and I use them to make a difference in the world and in the lives of others.
4. I know my core values, which are central to my purpose and how I live.
5. I believe that I have a higher purpose in life than merely making a living and having fun.
6. I am clear about my passions in life, expressing them through my work and my activities.
7. I have transformed my pain to make a difference in the lives of others; I have identified the pain and problems in the world that I am committed to addressing.
8. I can articulate my life purpose.
9. I consistently live with my life purpose day-in and day-out.
10. I regularly take ownership of how I am living my purpose and how I can live it more fully.

Scoring: Add up your per-question points and refer to the scoring below:

40-36: Congratulations – You are living life to its fullest and embody your life purpose at a high level.

35-30: Doing Well – You are well on your way to realizing your life purpose. With additional focus, you can align your lifestyle with your life purpose.

29-25: Opportunity – You have an opportunity to experience life at a higher level and the rewards of finding purpose.

24 or less: Wake-up Call – You are unaware of your purpose and most likely not feeling great about your life. This is your time and opportunity to re-focus, re-organize, and re-discover yourself.

PART 1

Unlocking Your Life Purpose

CHAPTER 2

Golden Key #1: People
Deciding Who You Truly Are

Chapter Overview

As far back as we can remember, our lives and opinions have been influenced by others: parents, relatives, teachers, role models, friends, partners, even one-off interactions. We have a chance to learn valuable life-lessons from every person we meet. We simply have to go from being influenced to actively learning from our influences.

Often, however, we are not consciously aware of the impact of these influences on our lives. Without this awareness, we cannot make effective conscious decisions about who we want to become.

My father had a profound impact on my life-decisions. He was a kind, intuitive, and respectful man. I loved being around him. One summer morning, he got into the family car without saying where he was going or why. Without asking, I hopped in the backseat.

My father drove to a small hamlet called Judson, about two miles from our farm. Even that tiny village had a wrong side of the tracks.

We stopped near a small tar-paper shack, much less a home, which crammed a family of nine--including seven children. I saw then that my father had brought sustenance to that struggling family, baskets of garden vegetables and meat he had butchered. I knew that no one had requested my father's help. No one had told him to take food to this family. I realized that he had done so as a caring person and a good Christian. In that moment, I made a conscious decision.

I decided that when I grew up, I wanted to be a kind and caring person like my father. I decided, on that day, to dedicate my life to helping others however I could.

My mother, too, provided me with life lessons. In many ways she was a great role model, looking after the family, cooking, keeping a tidy and attractive home, taking good care of her appearance, setting an excellent example as a woman. On the other hand, she often seemed distant and preoccupied with personal concerns. At times she would verbalize her frustration aloud, creating anxiety for me and likely for herself.

Again, I faced a moment of conscious decision-making. Who did I want to become? What did I stand for? I decided, based on my mother's influence, that I would learn to be different. I strove instead to become a more positive and loving person, devoted to helping others.

I am thankful to my mother for this life-lesson and for many others. Knowing what not to do is sometimes more important than knowing what to do.

My inclination for positivity has at times challenged me and my views. In a few cases, it has been detrimental to success in the traditional sense. I have overlooked warning signs in relationships and business dealings. I have trusted too much and too quickly. That said, I wouldn't have it any other way.

The inner-peace of being a positive person far outweighs the obstacles in the way, which are really just learning lessons and opportunities for growth. Being positive doesn't mean not dealing with negativity. It simply means re-channeling and redirecting negativity, worries, and concerns into more positive outlets, activities, and applications. It's a skill that takes time and practice like any other skill. Consider the examples below.

Persons	Behaviour	Example	My Life Decision
Father	Kind, caring, helpful	Brought food to a family in need	Be a caring, kind person who helps people
	Respectful of everyone	Treated everyone with respect, including those ridiculed by others	Treat everyone with respect
	Not standing up for himself and family	His siblings took advantage of him	Stand up for myself and family
	Openness to new ideas and innovations	Bought new and innovative products	Appreciate new ideas and innovation

Mother	Cared for her family	Prepared nutritious food, etc.	Care for my family
	Took good care of the home	Clean, tidy and attractive home	Create a nice home environment
	Cared for herself as a woman	Personal hygiene, skin care and dress	Take care of myself and appearance
	Verbally and physically non-expressive of love	Busy with household duties; did not express feelings	Be a loving person and express my feelings of love and care to others
	Preoccupied and distant	Did not give children attention	Despite the busy-ness of life, give people attention, especially children
	Verbalized anger and frustration	Verbally expressed anger and frustration	Be a positive and loving person

Life decisions I made about who I want to be

- Be a generous, caring, and helpful person.
- Make a meaningful difference in the lives of others.
- Be a positive and loving person.

My friend Anne is another example of someone who faced and made conscious life decisions. Her mother verbally abused her, repeatedly reminding Anne that she was stupid, worthless, destined for nothing and nowhere. Assaulted by this adversity, Anne courageously made a life decision to become the antidote to her abusers. She decided she would be their opposite. She would help children discover that they are smart and beautiful.

Anne's father loved her but did not protect her from her mother. He evaded the issue altogether, working long hours to be away from home. Again, Anne decided she would be the opposite. She would protect her children.

Anne's grandparents taught her essential life-skills and wisdom that she in turn passed onto many children. From her aunts, independent women working in the Northwest Territories, she learned to go where she could make a meaningful difference: to be of service. Her grandparents also taught her practical, day-to-day skills like sewing and lighting fires.

Persons	Behaviour	Example	My Life Decision
Mother	Verbally abusive	Told me I was stupid and worthless	Help children discover they are smart and wonderful
Father	Did not protect children from abusive mother	Worked long hours	Protect children
Aunts	Independent	Worked in NW territories	Go where you can make a difference
	Service minded – wanted to make difference	Worked with people in NW	Be of service
	Adventurous	Told stories about their adventures	Be adventurous
Grandparents	Taught me practical skills	Sewing, lighting fires	Help children learn and discover they can do things.

Anne's conscious life decisions about who she wanted to be:

- Convey value to children, make them feel beautiful.
- Protect children from abusive persons.
- Go where you can make a difference in the lives of others.
- Be adventurous and explore.

We are all of us combinations of various behaviours, ranging from self-empowering to self-destructive. Each of us has a conscious decision to make. Who do you want to become? It all starts there, with that question.

We must make decisions about our future, because if we do not then others else will. Influence will always be there to work us over if we allow it to, if we continue without a plan of our own. To learn, to grow, to discover ourselves requires conscious decision making. The best part? You get to create yourself and your future, one decision at a time.

When we point the lens at ourselves, when we stop living based on perceptions and start living based on personal experience through learning, then we make the best of our time with the key, influential persons in our lives.

Behaviors are values in Action
Application Exercise: What have I learned from others?

1. In the **Persons** column below, list the individuals who have had a profound impact on your life.
2. In the **Behaviours** column, list the behaviour(s) you noticed in these impactful persons.
3. In the **Example** column, list one specific example of the behaviours you observed.

4. In the **Your Life Decision** column, list the conscious life decisions you made about yourself by observing the examples of others.

Persons	Behaviour	Example	Your Life Decision

5. What kind of person have you decided to become based on your conscious life decisions?
    Example: I choose to be a kind, caring, and respectful person who is loving and positive in my relationships and interactions with others.

6. What have you learned about what is important to you in other areas of your life?

For each area of your life, as you consider what you don't like or don't want, equally consider what you do like and do want for yourself.

Then, articulate what you value in each area of your life.

Dislike	Like	What I Value
Work/Work Environment		
Career/Job		
Relationships		
Activities		
Home/home		
Other		

In summary, what do you most value?

_____

What does this tell you about your life purpose?

_____

"Memories of our lives, of our works and our deeds will continue in others."

\- Rosa Parks

Further Reflections

As we evolve and continue to learn about ourselves, we often gain insights about our role models, who we are, and how well our early life decisions are working for us.

"The 5 Languages of Love" by Dr. Gary Chapman, teaches that people have a preferred way of expressing love in relationships and how they want love shown to them.

1. Words of affirmation – using words to build up the other person. "Thanks for making dinner and cleaning up afterwards." Not – "It's about time you did some cooking and cleaning up. I am not your maid."
2. Gifts – a gift says, "He was thinking about me. Look what he got for me. Such a wonderful surprise."
3. Acts of Service – doing something for your partner that you know they would like. Taking out the garbage, vacuuming floors, and helping out are acts of service.
4. Quality time – giving your partner your undivided attention. Taking a walk together, or sitting on the couch with the TV off – talking and listening.
5. Physical touch – holding hands, hugging, kissing, and sexual intimacy are all expressions of love.

Of these five, each of us has a primary love language that speaks more deeply to us than all the others. Discovering our love language and the language of others, and effectively speaking it, is the best way to keep love alive and thriving in personal relationships.

Growing up, my father was a physically expressive parent. When he came in the door, he would light up and show he was happy to see me. As children, we would often sit on the arm of his big leather chair, and the younger children would sit on his lap. I liked holding his big hand when we were in church. In my heart, I knew he loved me, even though he was not verbally expressive, or using words of affirmation.

My mother showed her love through acts of service, ensuring my sister and I were always well dressed and encouraged us to try new things like piano and modelling lessons.

She also gave each of us wonderful Christmas presents. Somehow, she would know what I would like more than I myself would know, which was her expression of love. Although she did not express her love through physical touch or words of affirmation, I realized my mother expressed her love through acts of service, by giving us gifts, and by allowing us to be ourselves, to be children, and to pursue our lives.

I know that I was loved, which deepens my resolve to remain a loving person.

CHAPTER 3

Golden Key #2: Pain
Transforming Pain
Turning Scars into Stars

"I do not believe that sheer suffering teaches.
If suffering alone taught, all the world would be wise, since everyone
suffers. To suffering must be added mourning, understanding,
patience, love, openness and the willingness to remain vulnerable."
- Anne Morrow Lindberg
Author and wife of Charles Lindberg
American aviator, author, and the spouse of fellow Charles
Lindberg (June 22, 1906 – February 7, 2001)

In this chapter, you will identify the pain you have experienced or
seen, discovering the lessons it has in store for you. You will learn
how to be at peace with your pain and use it to make a meaningful
difference in your life and in the lives of others.

Transforming Your Pain
When I wrote the above heading, I asked myself, "Is pain a human
experience? If so, why? And where does it come from?"

These are profound questions, if I may say so, and could very well lay the foundation for another book. This book, however, examines and reveals how we can transform our pain.

Helen Keller discovered the transformative gift of her pain after years of struggle. Her blindness and speech limitations, she learned, were in fact her strengths. She said, "Character cannot be developed in ease and quiet. Only through experience of trial and suffering can the soul be strengthened, ambition inspired, and success achieved." True to her words, Keller transformed her pain to become a renowned educator to the blind and deaf.

Pain can also be identified and understood through the emotional wounds we experience. The path to your purpose or calling often emerges after you reflect upon your emotional wounds with a calm and clear mind.

Wherever your pain is, that is where your genius will be.

Finding genius within pain is a special skill that can be learned, that can forge our unique identity. This is a vital step in forming, solidifying, and sharing our purpose with the world.

Helen Keller's blindness, for example, became her genius. With it, she discovered how to communicate, how to live, and then how to teach others. Keller used her pain to liberate herself. Then she freed others from the same pain.

There is a direct correlation between your pain and your genius. When you stop running from your pain, accept it, and share it openly in service to others, you will inspire others. They, too, will want to experience your journey and find purpose by means of your purpose.

Pain comes in various forms – physical, emotional, spiritual, financial, and many more. The question is, what do we do with it? I have friends who say difficulties are inevitable but misery is optional. How do you see life?

Our attitudes and conscious decisions determine whether we experience life as misery or as difficulties that can summon our inner-genius.

> *"Our ultimate freedom is the right and power to decide how anybody or anything outside ourselves will affect us."*
> - Stephen R. Covey, Author and Speaker

Anne grew up with a verbally abusive mother, who told her she was stupid and worthless. Anne's parents got married when and because her mother became pregnant. Expressing her resentment at the decision, and at Anne, her mother would say, "If it wasn't for you..." She cast such abusive behaviour toward Anne but not toward her three younger siblings, who could do no wrong in the eyes of her mother.

Her father worked long hours to avoid his wife, leaving Anne and her siblings at their mother's mercy. To make matters worse, Anne's school teachers also called her stupid. Now, as an adult, Anne recognizes that her mother was bipolar, and that those teachers were simply not qualified to handle her special educational needs. To deflect attention away from their lack of capacity to teach children with special needs, they pointed the finger at Anne.

During her teenage years, years of blossoming youth, Anne's mother cut her hair short and refused to let her wear cosmetics. This made boys and socializing uncomfortable territory for Anne. In contrast, her younger sisters suffered no such constraints.

After high school, Anne found herself in a broken relationship. When she told her boyfriend that she wanted to part ways, he raped her. When Anne told her mother, she threw her out of the house, calling her "damaged goods."

With no place to go and no roof above, Anne resorted to living with the boyfriend who had violated her. She later married him out of fear and pressure from her mother.

Over the next few years, Anne's husband continued to physically abuse her. She learned that he was a first-generation survivor of abusive residential schools. He had been re-enacting the abuse placed upon him by his parents, abuse he had survived physically but carried emotionally.

Despite all she had suffered and faced, what were Anne's life decisions? She courageously decided to make a meaningful difference in the lives of others by:

- Communicating to children that they are smart
- Lighting a fire of hope within children
- Having compassion for residential school survivors and victims

Another incredible example of transforming pain into purpose comes from an 18-year-old Canadian. He was diagnosed with a malignant tumour in his right leg, which was amputated 15 centimetres (6 inches) above the knee. The night before his amputation procedure, Terry Fox read about an amputee runner. Inspired, he dreamt of running, too, not just for himself but for all persons with cancer.

Two years after the surgery, Terry began training for his Marathon of Hope, a cross-Canada run to raise money for cancer research and awareness. He ran over 5,000 kilometres (3,107 miles).

After 143 days and 5,373 kilometres (3,339 miles), Terry stopped running just outside Thunder Bay, Ontario. As fate would have it, his primary cancer had spread to his lungs. Disease may have taken his body, but it could not dimmish his spirit, which inspires many to this day.

In addition to running across Canada, Terry's goal was to raise a million dollars. drew people's conscientiousness, raising over 10 million dollars. He showed others how to help find a cure for cancer even when it had them cornered. To date, the Terry Fox marathons have raised over $700 million for cancer research. His name and his purpose will live on.

> *"I guess that one of the most important things I've learned is that nothing is ever completely bad. Even cancer - it's made me a better person. It's given me the courage and a sense of purpose I never had before. But you don't have to do like I did; wait until you lose a leg or get some awful disease before you take the time to find out the kind of stuff of which you're made. You can start now. Anybody can".*
> - Terry Fox

What stronger person is there than the person who transforms personal pain to make a positive difference in the lives of others? Take Sandy Lightner, for example. After a drunk driver killed her daughter, she responded and reacted by founding Mothers Against Drunk Driving (MADD).

Numerous similar scenarios show medical research programs established to find cures after the loss of children. Educational programs to help young people are often established by those who did not have the benefit of participating in a sport, skill, or academic pursuit.

Another example is Abel Bosum, a Cree leader from the community of Ouje-Bouboumou in Northern Quebec. Abel championed the fight to win recognition for his people and to secure territory for them.

For decades, the Ouje-Bouboumou Crees were forced to move time and again, driven to one area after another. All that because minerals were discovered in their traditional territory. Industry sought to uproot the Ouje-Bougoumou people from their home immemorial. Abel and other Cree leaders campaigned tirelessly to secure recognition for the Ouje-Bougoumou people as a nation, and for their right to territory.

Yet another example is Ryan Herjlac, a young Canadian boy who decided, at the age of 7, to do something to help other children who were dying from a lack of clean drinking water.

After hearing about the water problem at some schools, a concerned Ryan decided to raise enough money to build a well for <u>one</u> community in Africa. Young though he was, he worked hard to earn the $70 construction cost for the well. Upon reaching his goal and arranging for the well to be built, Ryan learned that $70 was enough only for a hand well. For a well deep enough and big enough to supply the entire community, he needed a lot more money.

Undaunted, Ryan kept at his dream. As word spread about his perseverance, others in his community were inspired to help him realize his dream. When he had raised $2000, he asked for the well to be built near a school so that children could access clean drinking water. The Angolo Primary School in northern Uganda became the home of 'Ryan's Well'.

Out of this dream, "Ryan's Well Foundation" was born.

To date, the foundation has completed 1148 water projects in numerous developing countries, constructed 1,255 latrines, and educated people on the importance of good hygiene. It has also provided 1 million persons with access to clean water. (www.ryanswell.ca)

After learning about the plight of schools in Africa, Ryan decided to do something about it. He started small, inviting others to help make a difference, from a five-year-old Floridan girl who sent him five cents of chore-money to a man from Dubai who donated five thousand dollars. Ryan has inspired many young children into believing that they, too, can change the world one act at a time.

Most examples of transforming pain do not go public like the ones above. A friend of mine lost her mother at the age of 12. By the time I met her, she was a foster mother to children in their teens. Affectionately called Aunt Lil, she transformed many lives through her loving care.

This circle of love and kindness included my son for after-school supervision, so that he would not return to an empty house in a new neighbourhood after his father and I had separated. Hiring Lillian was one of the best decisions I have ever made. She not only looked out for my son, she also helped me personally and in business. Lillian transformed the pain of losing a mother to help children in their teens who had suffered the same and many others.

In the previous chapter, I mentioned my father bringing food to a family in need. Years later, I told this turning-point story to my youngest brother, who, to my surprise, informed me that my account was nothing out of the ordinary. Our father, he said, would regularly take food to families in need. I suppose he was like a secret food Santa and knew who needed food. He just knew, somehow.

Like Aunt Lil, my father had a kind and caring heart, as do countless persons who continue to inspire humanity toward a brighter future.

Parents often strive to help children avoid the hardships they themselves had endured. My mother, for example, grew up in a low-income home. She toiled long hours for a room-and-board to attend high school. That experience drove her to ensure that my sister and I always had beautiful clothing, the means to look our best, and all the opportunities that she did not have.

I grew up in the original homeland of the Dakota people in Southern Minnesota. My mother recalled stories about how my great paternal grandfather had acquired the land, and how his wife and he had traded baked goods for meat with the Dakotas.

As a child, I was curious about the Dakotas, about what happened to them, where they went and why. A local museum housed some artefacts, but they couldn't answer my may questions. I began learning about Southern Minnesota's past, about the unjust history of the Dakotas losing their beloved lands and being banished from the state.

After my voluntary involvement in community development and cross-cultural projects, a major management consulting firm hired me to work on a project with the Crees from the James Bay in Northern Quebec. My objective was to assist with the implementation of one of the first modern treaties.

For reasons I am still discovering, I have been drawn over the years to projects involving Indigenous peoples. Perhaps it is because I believe we all have a right to determine our futures. Indigenous peoples, moreover, have inherent rights because of their ancient history in North America.

As a consultant, I provide services that assist leaders and organizations in determining their futures, in making sound decisions for themselves by developing and implementing plans to realize their dreams.

These examples have something in common. These persons all found a way through their pain to help others heal. The suffering of others around the world is readily available for us to see. I choose to see it as a readily available call to action. I choose to direct my focus and my energy toward making a positive difference in the lives of others.

What will you decide to do with your pain?

Pain and Difficulties Do Not Have to Be Personal

If you haven't experienced pain in the form of loss, fear, abandonment, breach of trust, or if you have already transformed your pain, you have the opportunity to select and transform another pain in the world.

Ask yourself, what pain in the world would you like to eliminate?

> *"Were there none who were discontented with what they
> have, the world would never reach anything better."*
> - Florence Nightingale

Application Exercise: How can you transform your pain or suffering to make a positive difference in the world?

- What pain or suffering have you personally experienced or seen?

- What, if anything, was missing in your childhood? What did you not receive from your caretakers that you are still seeking?
- What lessons have you learned from these experiences?
- What strengths have you gained from these experiences?
- Whom could you help with what you have learned?
- Are you ready to let go of pain and transform it into positivity?
- What pain or injustice do you see in your community or the world at large that you care deeply about?

Summary: What positive difference would you like to make in the lives of others?

_____

_____

_____

"Although the world is full of suffering, it is also full of the overcoming of it".
- Helen Keller, US blind & deaf educator (1880 – 1968)

CHAPTER 4

Golden Key #3: Proven Skills
Recognizing Your Talents and Abilities

"We must believe that we are gifted for something, and that this thing, at whatever cost, must be attained."
- Marie Curie (1867–1934)
French physicist and chemist, two-time Nobel Prize winner.

This chapter will give you the opportunity to acknowledge your abilities and talents. You will learn how to use your gifts to make a positive difference in the lives of others.

The Importance of Work

Work is vital. It's an expression of our purpose, talents, and abilities. According to *The Reinvention of Work* by Matthew Fox, work comes from the inside out and is an expression of our inner-self. He moreover describes work as an expression of our spirit within the world.

Work connects us with others at an interpersonal level and at a higher level: service to the world. Purpose-driven work is about so much more than just a paycheck.

Philosopher and theologian Thomas Aquinas taught that we discover our "calling" by following our natural inclinations, using our talents and abilities to find joy in our lives.

Modern philosophers Joseph Campbell and Bill Moyers expressed a similar notion, advocating that we should "follow our bliss." Fox believes that without bliss in our work and without passion for what we do, we have not yet found our work. We might have a job, but not our calling.

When you find work that reveals, engages, and empowers your talents in a sustainable way, you will have found your calling. When that moment happens, you will know it to be true.

You will then be operating at the highest level, doing purpose-driven work.

Affirm or Reconfirm Your Skills and Abilities

We readily recognize that each creature on Earth has a unique nature and purpose, but many of us do not yet recognize our own talents and abilities.

Society seldom encourages us to be aware of our inner-genius or to affirm our gifts. Most schools and many workplaces emphasize conformity and fitting in. The media herds us and our children into a similar thought-enclosure. All too often, career and work choices are based on what pays best, not on what makes the best of us.

"Our greatest fear is not that we are inadequate, but that we are powerful beyond measure", according to Marianne Williamson. In other words, we fear the world's expectations if we embraced our abilities and unlocked our potential. Some of us even believe that we are unique in hosting this fear, unlike countless others who also have not harnessed their talents.

Even still, there abound shining and hopeful examples of self-reflection leading to profound realizations of inner-talent and skill.

I recently spoke with the website manager at one of Canada's leading technology companies. We discussed his perspective on the company after passing the 8-month mark in his employment. He had just launched a major restructuring of the company's website and its nearly 3,000 products.

As he spoke excitedly about freshly-finished revisions and about key initiatives on the horizon, he paused to consider that his current role required almost every aspect of his professional background.

With great excitement, he said the challenges faced required all the knowledge and skills he had acquired over the years. He realized that it took every past challenge he had tackled to develop the technical, strategic, managerial, and creative problem-solving skills required for the complexity of his current role.

It occurred to him that all his past experiences had helped him hone his skills for the present. They had shaped him and prepared him for greater challenges, for what lay ahead. At that moment, it became undeniable that a seemingly random set of experiences had chiseled him into someone who was unusually well-adapted for his current role, where he could make a positive difference.

Let's revisit Anne. As a child, she was artistically inclined, finding joy and comfort in drawing and reading stories. As an adult, Anne sought to instill the same feelings of comfort and safety in the lives of her children. During her second marriage, she chose home-schooling for her two daughters, thereby protecting them from the possibility of bullying and negative experiences.

When, as a mature adult, Anne returned to school, her daughters returned to public schooling and placed ahead of their classmates in the same grades. Their upbringing had done its part.

After graduating, Anne started work as a Graphic Designer. After the initial spark of landing a new job began to fade, she realized that she did not particularly enjoy sitting in a cubicle. She struggled to find purpose in her work and soon sought something different.

In the meantime, Anne took up cleaning at a private group home. There she met residents from the North, gaining new perspectives and weighing new possibilities. Shortly afterward, the Frontier Foundation hired her to work in a Northern Ontario school. Her daughters, whom she had raised to think and live independently, supported her decision.

Anne completed an online course to earn an educational assistant diploma. The school extended her 10-month contract to five years. For the very first time, she felt accepted by her community's many cultures. She made friends with the Elders and found purpose in working with children. She had a feeling of adventure but felt right at home.

As funding dried up for Anne's contract, she accepted an opportunity to teach at a Southern Ontario Indigenous school. Anne delights in helping children realize that they are smart and capable of skills ranging from sewing to digital movie production.

Ellen Violette, a highly regarded writer and 'getting-published' coach, grooved with the music business for years. When the industry changed, she tried her hand at real estate but found that it wasn't for her.

She then turned to writing and discovered her inner-talent. More importantly, she liked it! Ellen used her gift to start a highly regarded eBook Coaching practice, helping other aspiring writers draft, complete, and publish their books.

I have personally experienced moments when I felt "this is what I am here to do." In those moments, all the various experiences of my life have come together to help me accomplish something far greater.

Some people refer to this as mindset "being in the zone." I call it being in my own time zone. Past concerns and future worries no longer exist. Now becomes everything.

Sport psychology consultant Karlene Sugarman describes "being in the zone" as immersed in the flow, a mental state where a person is focused, involved, and successful in carrying out an activity.

It's like finding your mojo, being on a roll. You are so engaged in the activity that nothing else seems to matter. You are present, undistracted, and connected to your task.

What do People Say You are Good at?

Professionally_____

_____

_____

_____

Personally _____

_____

_____

_____

Identifying Your Skills and Abilities

"Being in the zone" requires the ability to meet challenges and take positive action. In developing the skills required to overcome obstacles, you naturally learn how to take the necessary actions. As with the website manager above, your talents can give you clues about your life-purpose.

Ask yourself, "What are my talents and abilities?" To discover your gift, think about situations where you were in "the zone," delighted by what you did and how you performed, proud of yourself and the results. Think back to when you found fulfillment and happiness in what you did.

What were you doing?

_____

_____

_____

_____

_____

_____

_____

See my personal and professional examples of skills and abilities, below:

Situation – What did you do?	Results	Skills/Abilities Used
As a volunteer, engaged visitors in learning about history and culture	Visitors left delighted	Interpersonal, teaching, and training skills
Helped professional clients find synergy and see the bigger picture	Plans included everyone's ideas	Facilitation, strategic-thinking and systems knowledge and skills

Developed innovative staff training programs to positively shift attitudes	Staff adapted their attitudes and behaviours so that clients received good care	Needs assessment, program design, collaboration, and innovative thinking

Before attempting the Application Exercise below, there is one more step to consider about yourself. Even as there are many things you are good at, there might be several things at which you are not skilled.

Equally important as knowing our talents is knowing what they are not. By seeing both sides of the coin, we can determine what not to pursue and where we should wholeheartedly focus our energy and time.

My (Partial) List of Not-talented Areas

- At 9 years old, learned I was not good at cutting my own hair; decided not to cut my hair or anyone else's
- Discovered I am not interested in being a mechanic and will not fix cars
- Realized I do not want to fix teeth and be a dentist
- I would not make a good accountant
- Nor a graphic artist
- Nor a copy editor

What about you? What have you discovered that you are not good at?

_____

_____

_____

Exercise: What Are Your Skills and Abilities?

To start the exciting search for your skills and abilities, recall a few situations where you were highly pleased with your results or when you were in "the zone." What were you doing?

Situation – What did you do?	Results	Skills/Abilities Used

Many of us have more skills and abilities than we believe or give ourselves credit for. In *The Success Principle*, Jack Canfield says most persons believe that others are better at things than they are. As a result, we tend to think more about what we cannot do than what we can do. This creates a negative state of mind that drains the energy we need to make a positive difference in the world. Is there a solution?

To enhance and expand your thinking about skills and abilities, I suggest ordering *"The New Quick Job-Hunting Map,"* developed by Malcolm Knowles. This e-booklet allows you to explore your skillset, identifying the skills you most enjoy in three major categories:

1. People – all types of persons, as well as individuals with specific backgrounds
2. Information or Data – knowledge, data, ideas, facts, figures, statistics
3. Things – physical objects, instruments, tools, machinery, equipment, vehicles, materials

Knowles' guide and similar references can help you recognize your abilities. They provide a framework for positive action that allows you, the action-taker, to find pieces of yourself and your life-purpose.

For many years, my husband and I moved every few years. In each new city, I sought and found employment while he continued working with the organization that had transferred us. Each time we moved, I saw an opportunity to refresh my skills and abilities. I turned each move into an episode of self-discovery, learning what I wanted to do more of and less of and where I could make a positive difference.

Reflect on Your Accomplishments

To attain clarity on your talents, try reflecting on your achievements. Start by making a list of your professional and personal triumphs. For each item on your list, identify the skills you leveraged to accomplish them. See examples, below:

My Examples

Accomplishments	Skills/Abilities Used
Designed and facilitated planning sessions resulting in improved results and alignment within the organization	Planning, facilitation, interpersonal skills
Conceptualized innovative healthcare programs for women and teenagers aimed at heightened responsibility for personal health	Collaboration, strategic thinking, change management

Designed and facilitated a breakthrough process that resulted in the client achieving their targets and creating the best performing division in its categories	Design, innovative thinking, planning and facilitation

Your Examples

Accomplishments	Skills/Abilities Used

What do people say you are good at?

_____

_____

_____

What do you know you are not good at?

_____

_____

_____

Integrating Talents and Abilities
with Your Life Purpose

Dorothy Grant, a well-known First Nations artist and fashion designer, provides a creative example of integrating talent with life-purpose. She combines 10,000-year-old legends of the Haida into high-fashion, fusing myth with flawlessly designed and manufactured garments. Drawing from ancient stories, Grant transforms age-old symbols into timeless clothing.

I recently spoke to a young woman about aligning talent with life-purpose. She said some of her friends intended to make money with their skills and pursue their purpose outside of work. Although some individuals use their jobs to make money primarily for non-work pursuits, many believe in a more holistic approach that integrates work with life-purpose.

When you harmonize your life-purpose with your work to make a positive difference in the world, you gain personal satisfaction and simultaneously benefit others, sometimes beyond your imagination.

Many individuals feel disconnected from their life-purpose and their soul's longing. The first step toward overcoming this mental rift is to acknowledge that life-purpose is available to us all. We need only to search in the right places.

This journey of self-discovery makes us realize that we have what it takes to live a purposeful life, using our abilities to make a difference.

Diverse Expression of Talents within Families

It is insightful and amazing to behold the diversity of talent that can exist within the same family. I am here reminded of two old friends, the late Grand Chief Billy Diamond and his brother the late

Albert Diamond, an entrepreneur and CEO from the Waskaganish community in the James Bay of Northern Quebec.

Billy, a skilled politician, became the political voice for the Cree Nation. He found his passion as a translator for Cree elders when the nine Cree communities sued the Province of Quebec. The elders sought to stop the province from proceeding with the James Bay Hydro-Electric project, the largest initiative of its kind. Billy's natural talent with words made him a formidable speaker, negotiator, and leader.

Albert Diamond established himself as an astute businessman by developing highly successful enterprises and joint ventures, and by supporting indigenous businesses across Canada. Discovering and applying innate talent ran through the Diamond family.

The late Chief Malcolm Diamond, their father, considered it essential for his children to seek education suitable for leaders. Gertie Diamond, their sister, pioneered First Nation education by making significant contributions. Charlie Diamond, their brother, chose to honour the traditional Cree way of life by becoming a skilled hunter and trapper. These Diamonds in turn raised talented children who likewise grew up to achieve great feats for the Cree.

As the Diamonds each had distinct talents, think about your own family members and how their abilities set them apart. Notice the diversity of talents and embrace each for its uniqueness.

Growing up, my sister loved creating from Plaster of Paris and my brother loved taking things apart to see how they worked. As adults, my sister started a successful ceramics business and my brother became a maintenance mechanic. In my formative years, I found inspiration in my father's altruism and service to others. Those memories of youth became the foundation for my true calling. I love teaching others about their unique talents and helping them discover their life-purpose.

Application Exercise: How can you use your abilities and talents to make a positive difference in the lives of others? Challenge yourself to be your best self.

As you consider your skills, talents, and triumphs, ask yourself: "What is most meaningful to me and my life purpose?"

_____

_____

_____

"We are not here to merely make a living. We are here to enrich the world, and we impoverish ourselves if we forget this errand".
- Woodrow Wilson

CHAPTER 5

Golden Key #4: Passion
Living Your Life with Passion

"Understand your purpose in life by feeling your heart's desires".
- Marcia Wieder

This chapter is about self-discovery. You will clarify what you care deeply about and want to do more often. In doing so, you will find pursuits that inspire a great sense of satisfaction, momentum, and rejuvenation. You will meet your 4th P: passion.

The dictionary defines passion as ardour, obsession, or excitement. Said another way, people who are passionate about their life-purpose simultaneously display a high level of commitment and excitement toward their work. They love love learning, talking about living their purpose in their work, and daily lives. They do well at what they do and find joy in striving to do even better.

I recall a tenacious man who planned to establish a garage in his Northern Ontario community. During his holidays, he would drive long hours to gas stations in Southern Ontario, determined to find information on optimal station setup and interest in a potential joint venture.

Those who are passionate about their purpose are relentless in pursuing it.

Photographer Edward Curtis provides another fine example of someone deeply dedicated to his purpose. He sought to document the 'old time Indian,' his dress, his ceremonies, his life, his manners. Curtis' goal, however, was not merely to photograph. It was to capture the essence of Native American Indian life the way it was before it disappeared. He worked tirelessly for years to photograph every tribe in North America.

From every field emerge champions and trailblazers who pursue their work with passion. Examples include chef Julia Childs, inventor Thomas Edison, automotive industrialist Henry Ford, and human rights activist Martin Luther King, to name a few. Nelson Mandela battled Apartheid and won. Mahatma Gandhi freed India from British rule through non-violent resistance. Jonas Salk found a cure for polio. The list goes on.

You might wonder, as I often have, how these individuals discovered their life-purpose. Upon reflection and careful study, you will find underlying patterns in their life-decisions.

They all found something they cared deeply about. They all began like any other unknown person from their generation. They all took one persistent step at a time in pursuing their passion. On the road that was undoubtedly difficult, they failed time and again but got back up and kept going. Along the way, they shared their enthusiasm and inspired others with their success. They voiced their concerns, projected their passion, and actively engaged those who supported their dreams. Eventually they found that elusive success reserved for those who see failure as learning and life as an opportunity to help others.

Mother Teresa, for instance, started her career by teaching children in India. She became increasingly disturbed by the poverty and ensuing misery surrounding her throughout Calcutta. While soul searching, she made a decision to leave the convent and help the poor by living among them. She felt her inner-calling.

Bolstered in her efforts by a group of young women, Mother Teresa laid the foundations for a new religious community that helped the *"poorest among the poor."* Based on that experience, Mother Teresa advanced to her next initiative, opening her first home for the dying.

Like others who found life-purpose, Mother Teresa took one step at a time. Each step provided the momentum required for the next. Small triumphs led to bigger ones. In contrast, we sometimes dally about for years, hoping to memorize the entire map before beginning our journeys.

Think back to Anne once again. She, too, progressed one step at a time toward discovering her life-purpose, starting with homeschooling her children to protect them, then going back to school and excelling as an adult student.

Anne went on to make a positive difference by working in the Northwest Territories, where she expanded her areas of service from children to the community. After many steps and years of progress, she found her life-purpose: helping children shift their self-image from "I am stupid and can't do things" to "I am smart and capable."

Anne lives to light the fire of hope within children.

On a now-infamous day in Selma, Alabama, a then-unknown African American woman refused to yield her bus seat to a white man. She was tired of constantly trudging to the back of the bus like a second-class

American. That day, she had no intention of starting the Civil Rights Movement. She wanted simply to keep her bus seat, but that simple act of resistance catalyzed the Movement.

The Rosa Parks story gave new life to the African American voice and ignited the slumbering passions of many others ethnicities. Rosa lit the fire. Empathy fanned the flame.

> *"Stand for something, or you will fall for anything.*
> *Today's mighty oak is yesterday's nut that held its ground."*
>   - Rosa Parks

Know What Brings You Joy and Satisfaction

Recap what you have learned about yourself:

- What kind of activities, pursuits, causes, and situations do you care deeply about?
- What touches your heart and calls out to you?
- What kind of work has given you great satisfaction and innately calls you back to it?
- If money were not an issue, what would you love to do?

Application Exercise: Clarify what you most deeply care about. As you consider what you care about, what calls to you?

_____

_____

_____

> *"What are some of your brave, beautiful, and brilliant ideas? How*
> *do you want to make things better for yourself? Your loved ones, your*
> *community and the world? What would you do if you ran the world?"*
>   - Shelly Rachanow

CHAPTER 6

Golden Key #5: Putting It Together
The Master Key to Your Life-Purpose

"I am here for a purpose and that purpose is to grow into a
mountain, not to shrink to a grain of sand. Henceforth I will
apply ALL my efforts to become the highest mountain of all
and I will strain my potential until it cries for mercy."
- Og Mandino 1923-1996

In the last four chapters you considered the other 4 'Ps':

People – What have you learned from others and whom have you become through that learning?

Pain – How can you transform your pain to better the lives of others? Or, what pain in the world calls to you to address it?

Proven Abilities and Skills – What skills and abilities do you have, or can develop, that can make a positive difference?

Passion – What do you care most deeply about?

In reality, the 4 Golden Keys discussed so far provide ways for you to discover your life-purpose and what is most meaningful to you. When you integrate what you have learned from these 4 Keys, you will discover the 5th and Master Key to unlocking and harnessing your life-purpose.

What have You Discovered about Your Life-Purpose?

- What kind of person do you want to be?
- What pain do you want to transform or address?
- What are you good at? What talents, abilities, and skills do you have? How can you use them to make a positive difference?
- What do you love to do? What brings you joy and satisfaction? What do you care deeply about?
- What difference do you want to make in your life and with your life? At the end of your journey, what do you want to have accomplished?

Put it All Together: Your Master Key, Your Life-Purpose

Write down the essential elements of your Master Key, integrating:

- The kind of person I want to be is...
- The pain in the world I want to ease is...
- I want to use my skills and abilities to...
- The difference I want to make is...

My Master Key Example:

Element #1: I want to be a loving person who finds joy and satisfaction in helping others.

Element #2: I assist indigenous people in determining their future and improving their business potential to ease the financial strain from a lack of economic development.

Element #3: I want to use my strategic planning, implementation and capacity building skills to carry out this endeavour.

Element #4: The difference I want to make is in the lives of others. I love helping people focus on what they want. I help them envision their purpose and a better future for themselves. With my guidance, they discover that they can achieve extraordinary results. They find the power and freedom to create their own lives and futures.

My Life-Purpose Example:

I place people on the path to unlocking and harnessing their life-purpose.

Application Exercise: What are Your 4 Master Key Elements?

_____

_____

_____

_____

Application Exercise: What is Your Life Purpose?

_____

_____

_____

_____

Life-Purpose Checklist

- Should be one sentence in length
- Should be easily understood by a twelve-year-old
- Should be easy to remember and state
- You may also wish to draw a symbol of your purpose

See more examples of people's life purpose on page 84.

Recall the words of George Bernard Shaw:

"This is the true joy in life—that being used for a purpose recognized by yourself as a mighty one. I am of the opinion that my life belongs to the whole community and as long as I live it is my privilege to do whatever I can. I want to be thoroughly used up when I die. The harder I work the more I live. I rejoice in life for its own sake. Life is no brief candle to me. It's a sort of splendid torch, which I've got to hold up for the moment and I want to make it burn as brightly as possible before handing it on to future generations."

PART 2

Living Your Purpose

CHAPTER 7

Choosing Empowering Beliefs

"Whatever the mind can conceive and believe, it can achieve."
- Napoleon Hill
Best Selling Author of Think and Grow Rich

Even as computers require updates to expand functionality and improve performance, so do we humans need to update our belief systems to attain success and elevate our lives.

In this chapter you will self-install 'Belief System 2.0,' thereby learning to choose empowering beliefs that allow you to fulfill your life-purpose.

Your brain is a powerful instrument, a mega-computer, but it can function only as effectively as its programming. 'Belief System 1.0,' the one we are upgrading, is frequently programmed with fear and based on limitation. Consequentially, it parades all the reasons you cannot live a purpose-driven life.

Let's look at the programming of Belief System 1.0. Which of the following Limiting Beliefs look familiar?

Limiting Beliefs

- I must know everything before trying something new.
- I might not succeed. I might fail.
- I might succeed, and then others would expect me to do more!
- Others might blame me if I make a mistake.
- Others might not regard my purpose as significant.
- Others might not like or understand my living a purpose-driven life.
- It's safer to do things the way I have always done them in the past.
- I don't have enough education to realize my purpose.

Your mind is profoundly potent. It can visualize, plan, and create your reality, delivering it to you day by day, action by action. If you can imagine it and believe in it, then its creation is possible. Your tenacity, your skills, and your persistence will slowly but surely turn that possibility into a probability. You will then experience the positive momentum of your actions, carrying you beyond your perceived fears and your limitations. You will then sense your inevitable success in the morning air.

I recently heard a twist on the statement "I will believe it when I see it." The truth is: "You will see it when you believe it."

What keeps you stuck in your old, self-limiting mindset created by Belief System 1.0? Our programming, which is mostly based on limited information from our four senses—sight, hearing, taste, and touch—frequently does not include spiritual beliefs.

There's a story about doctors studying the effects of arthroscopic knee surgery, who assigned patients with sore, worn-out knees to one of three surgical procedures: scraping of the knee joint, washing out the knees, or doing nothing.

During the 'doing nothing' surgeries, doctors anaesthetized the patients and made three surface-incisions on the knee, pretending to operate their surgical instruments. Several years later, patients who had the 'doing nothing' surgeries reported pain-relief like the patients who underwent an actual surgical procedure. How and why did that happen?

The mind believed that the surgery would improve the knee. The body acted as the brain instructed.

According to Neuroscientists who study expectancy theory, we spend our whole lives becoming conditioned. By experiencing a lifetime of events, your brain learns to expect or anticipate what will happen – whether it happens that way or not. Your mind contains years of "evidence" from your four senses.

By consciously expecting something to happen a particular way, your intentions and your thoughts get tangled in that outcome. This increases the likelihood that you will act or decide in the manner that attracts your oft-anticipated reality.

What about negative thoughts that seem to emerge from nowhere, randomly assailing us? These are beyond our control, but the actions we take when facing those thoughts are within our control.

Positive expectancy is vital to achieving the desired results. By updating your Belief System, you begin to believe what you want is possible. Then your mind begins to pool resources, ramp up operations, and function in a way that accomplishes the task for you!

"You can be anything you want to be, if only you believe with self-sufficient conviction and act in accordance with your faith; for whatever the mind can conceive and believe it can achieve".
- Napoleon Hill

Believe In Yourself

According to Jack Canfield, co-creator of Chicken Soup for the Soul, if want to create your dream life, you have to believe that you can make it happen. That belief is the irreplaceable foundation on which all your ideas, plans, and actions will stand.

Moreover, you need to believe that you have the right stuff, the skills needed for the mission, the drive to win. In other words, you have to believe in yourself.

Some call it self-esteem. Others call it self-confidence. It all comes down to a deep-seated belief that you have what it takes, that you have the abilities and talents to realize your life-purpose. That belief is your freedom to leave the legacy you wish to leave.

Your life-purpose will not land on your lap. It takes the journey of a lifetime to realize and express our life-purpose. Will you embark upon this incomparable adventure? None of us are destined for greatness unless we make it so through our decisions.

"Destiny is what happens to us. Freedom is what we do with it."
-Dain Supero, Yoga Teacher

"You weren't an accident. You weren't mass-produced. You weren't an assembly-line product. You were deliberately planned, specifically gifted, and lovingly positioned on Earth by the Master craftsman".
- Max Luado, another best-selling author.

Believing in yourself is an attitude, a decision to succeed. It is a way of being you can consciously develop with training and expert guidance. Although it helps to have parents or a community that provide positive support, many of us have received from our parents the same limiting beliefs they received from theirs. To use an old proverb, the apple seldom falls far from the tree.

Supported by vast professional and personal experience, I conclude that it is an adult responsibility to update our beliefs, to undergo an attitude makeover, to develop the skills needed to be a success.

You might have heard the saying, "If it is going to be; it's up to me!" I recently heard a related saying: no one can be you for you.

Jack Canfield talks about the common denominator in the hundreds of successful people he has interviewed. Almost each of them professed they were not the most gifted or talented in their fields but chose to believe that anything was possible, that they could make it happen. They also reported that they had studied, practiced, and worked harder than others, which eventually contributed to their success.

These winners didn't wait for destiny to make them winners. They exercised their freedom to make decisions, take actions, and create their own victories.

In *Outliers*, Malcolm Gladwell describes a few famous persons like Bill Gates, members of the Beatles, and several others who experienced tremendous success by investing over 10,000 hours of their lives into what they loved doing, resulting in becoming more and more skillful at it.

But time invested is not enough by itself. In addition to putting in the work, success requires acting as if all things are possible. By believing in yourself and the possibility of success, you will think, say, and do the things needed for your success.

The opposite also holds. If you believe something is impossible, you will not think, say, or do what is necessary to make it possible.

You are a self-fulfilling prophecy. Believe to achieve.

When you look at your life and your results, what attitudes have prevailed? What are your dominant beliefs?

Turning Self Limiting Beliefs (LB) Into Empowering Beliefs (EB)

Let's revisit the Self-Limiting Beliefs considered earlier in the chapter. Let's give you that Belief System 2.0 upgrade using Empowered Beliefs. As you explore and assess your Belief System, consider how these beliefs have influenced and shaped the course of your life.

Examples:

LB: I must know everything before trying something new.
EB: *I cannot know everything, but I can use what I know, and by trying I can learn more.*

LB: I might make a mistake and might fail.
EB: *It is okay to make mistakes and to learn from my failures.*

LB: I might not succeed.
EB: *I might not succeed at everything I try, but I am willing to learn and to persist.*

LB: I might succeed, but then others would expect me to do more.

EB: *I am willing to surprise myself! It is okay for me to set realistic expectations for myself despite what others think.*

LB: People might not appreciate that I live a purpose-driven life.

EB: *It is more important and joyous to do what I value than to worry about what others might appreciate. Everyone has a right to their preferences. I am responsible for mine.*

LB: Others might not like me if I make a mistake.

EB: *Everyone has a right to their opinion. It is none of my business what others think of me. Some will like what I do, some will not. It is essential that I love myself regardless of what others like or don't like.*

LB: Doing new things goes against the way we have always done in the past.

EB: *For me to grow, I permit myself to try new things as long as they don't conflict with my principles. I have learned and attempted new things and will continue to try them.*

LB: I don't have enough education to do what I want.

EB: *I may not have enough education right now, but I have what it takes to gain the knowledge I need to succeed.*

LB: I am just a...

EB: *I am at just the right age to take the next step. I am just right for whatever I want to try.*

> *"You have to believe in yourself when no one else*
> *does. That is what makes you a winner."*
> - Venus Williams, Olympic Gold Medal Winner

Application Exercise: How will you upgrade your Belief System? What Self-limiting Beliefs are holding you back? What is your new Empowering Belief to overcome each Self-limiting Belief?

My Self-Limiting Beliefs	New Empowering Beliefs

Notice how you feel when replacing a Self-Limiting Belief with an updated Empowering Belief. At times you might feel phony, like you're pretending and saying something that doesn't fit your current perception of reality. Belief System 1.0 is likely to clash with your new operating system. Be aware of this, expect it, and let these thoughts pass as you fully convert to Belief System 2.0.

As you are installing Belief System 2.0, your brain will ask if you want to update or retain your old beliefs. This is a defining moment of decision-making for you. This is your freedom to choose who you will become.

There are two thoughts that every successful person must learn to let go:

"I will never make it," and "I am already there."
- Yehunda Berg

CHAPTER 8

Using Failure as A Stepping Stone

Based on my experience and my observation of many successful persons, success necessitates taking risks, making mistakes, and learning from those vital experiences. This chapter explains the relationship between life-purpose and failure, or, as I call them, temporary setbacks.

You will undoubtedly encounter many a temporary setback in your journey. Knowing what to do when faced with failure is among the greatest skills you can learn. It will allow you to navigate perilous straits, stay on course, and sail triumphantly toward your life-purpose.

Learning from Failures or Mistakes
Kevin Sandy, a wonderful colleague, says in his Cayuga culture that the word failure does not exist. That is something to ponder.

Underlying that concept is the realization that we can learn as much from our failures as we can from our accomplishments—some say more so. Our mistakes, make no mistake, are indispensable learning experiences if we mine persistently for the golden veins buried within the ore. Most of us give up too soon, often stopping within days of striking gold without even knowing it.

Unfortunately, we often prefer to mentally and emotionally block the vital memories of our perceived failures. When we do think of them, we do so with disdain and not with the intent to improve. There is, however, a gold-mine of information we can glean from our failures if we search with the lens of learning.

We are familiar with stories of persons who courageously used failures as learning experiences:

- Thomas Edison persisted (and succeeded) despite more than 10,000 failed experimental attempts at creating a light bulb.
- Walt Disney failed in businesses numerous times, and was hardly taken seriously, before he made it.
- Colonel Sanders approached almost 1,000 restaurants owners attempting to sell his chicken recipe.
- Jack Canfield received nearly two hundred rejection letters before he sold his first book, Chicken Soup for the Soul.
- JK Rowling's Harry Potter book was rejected 12 times by publishers.
- 3M's discovery of 'post-it notes' emerged unexpectedly from a mistake and became the widely popular 3M adhesive product we use today.

Thousands of people have succeeded despite and because of their failures. Motivational speaker, Bob Kittel, author of *En-Lighten Up*, used failure to succeed by building on each failed attempt. Instead of shunning failure, he analysed it to take his next step.

He nostalgically recalls, "I wouldn't be where I am today if it weren't for my failures and where my failures led me. Success could be just a few failures away."

"I've lived, I've loved, I've lost, I've hurt, I've trusted.
I've made mistakes, but most of all I've learned."
- Source Unknown

A Few of My Examples

Mistakes (a few of the many)	Lesson Learned
Loaning money to people who promised to repay	Loan a small amount of money to test if you are repaid. If you are not, draw a red line and do not loan more to the individual
Taking on too much project work	Estimate time required for each project; add 30% contingency; improve project estimations
Trying to lead historical walks that required memorizing dozen of dates and facts without the assistance of notes	Take on interactive roles, not ones requiring memorization of volumes of data without notes

We must humbly acknowledge that we are not going to succeed at everything. Knowing what is not for us is equally as important as leveraging our talents and learning from our mistakes.

Sometimes what we call 'failure' is really just a necessary struggle called 'learning,' and what we call 'success' is the product of that learning.

Take the necessary time to reflect and recall some of your failures and what you learned from them. The lessons you take home are far more essential to finding life-purpose than the mistakes you leave on the road.

Your Examples

Mistakes	Lesson Learned

Dealing with Failure

Does any of this sound familiar?

- So, you were given an important assignment, and you struck out.
- The big trip produced no results.
- Your prospective client presentation wasn't a home run.
- The major sale went to a competitor.
- Your new recipe flopped.
- Your speech at the annual meeting fell flat.

What would you do upon hearing that? How would you react?

If you let your feelings rule, you will mentally crawl into a shell and stop striving for success. Naturally, that seems wrong and counter-productive to finding life-purpose. But how can you develop the "oomph" to get up and go to bat again?

First, consider these bits of wisdom from managers who have been there:

- A mistake proves that someone stopped procrastinating long enough to do something.
- In sports, they say that winning seldom proves anything. You have to fall on your face to get a chance to show what you are made of.
- Reminder: winners lose more often than losers. That's because they try more times. But one success can make up for many failures.

> *"Every failure is a step to success."*
> *- William Whell*

Second, recall your mistakes and where you fell short of victory. More important, consider what you learned from those experiences instead of sweeping them under the rug.

Remember New York Mayor Fiorello LaGuardia's classic line: "When I make a mistake it's a beauty."

Third, think up three new ideas fast and go to work on them right away. Don't look back. Put your eyes on the road ahead.

Many successful companies encourage risk-taking. That does not mean viewing foolish risks as a prescription for success. But it does mean that calculated risks must be factored into business decisions. More than that, such risks should be acted upon when the potential results, or the lessons learned, could be game-changers.

How do you decide if a risk is worth taking? Consider the worst possible outcomes first. Decide whether such results would be bearable or destructive. If the latter is more likely, forego the risk. Otherwise, assess carefully the benefit associated with the risk through risk-benefit analysis. By following such a process, the risk becomes a calculated move based on objective fact rather than subjective opinion.

Whenever a plan goes wrong, learn from it. Don't hide it or from it. Do it better the second time because of the lessons from the first time. Use failure as a stepping stone, because if you stop trying it can become a gravestone.

> *"Failure brings victory. Surrender brings defeat"*
> *- Dain Supero, Yoga Teacher*

Excerpt from Personal Report for the Executive. Year unknown

> *"Success seems to be connected with ACTION. Successful people keep moving. They make mistakes, but they DON'T QUIT."*
> *- Conrad Hilton*

Bonus Tip: Keep and cherish persons in your life who always see the best in you. I recall once feeling down like a grand failure, a feeling I explained to my then 10-year-old son. His words lifted me right up. "You are a big success to me," he said. I asked him to write it on a paper, so I would have it as a reminder. I have kept this small treasure on my desk for over 40 years.

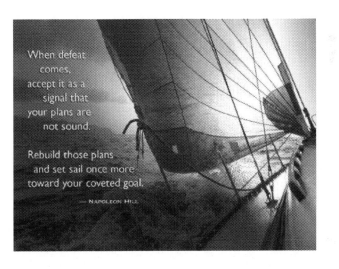

When defeat
comes,
accept it as a
signal that
your plans are
not sound.

Rebuild those plans
and set sail once more
toward your coveted goal.

— NAPOLEON HILL

BONUS CHAPTER 9

Accelerate Living Your Life-Purpose

"Most people are so busy knocking themselves out trying to do everything they think they should, they never get around to do what they want to do".
- Kathleen Winsor
1919-2003, Author

Having found your 4 Ps, your Master Key, and your life-purpose, you should naturally be curious about the next step in your evolution. That next step is the focus of this chapter.

In the sections that follow, you will create a plan to manifest your life-purpose. You will identify short-term action steps and determine your long-term plan.

Moving Forward

For some, these next steps will be a continuation of current actions with added acceleration. For others, it may require a bigger personal and professional leap, requiring more planning and effort.

Wherever you are is the perfect place! The key is to get moving — which requires deciding what to do.

Tips

- If you can think small or think Big – You might as well think BIG!
- Envision the difference you want to make.
- Be clear about your purpose – clarity is power.
- You get there one step at a time – what are the three things you can do each week and schedule in the coming week?
- Each step will lead you to the next, and the next one, and the next one.
- Believe it first – then you will see it. Our limiting beliefs block our success. Believe that it is possible, and it is more likely to be so.
- You can do anything – visualize it and take action.
- You have the power to harness your thoughts and choose Empowering Beliefs.
- Your intention creates a physical reaction in your body, and with certainty it will happen.
- Think about your purpose and how it will help others – when you serve others, you are more powerful and will attract the resources you need to realize your objectives.
- Set crystal clear goals, so that your brain can focus what success will look like to achieve it.
- The most important factor that separates winners from losers is that winners take action!
- Surround yourself with positive and supportive people who believe in you.
- Take action each day.

> *"Nothing is worth more than this day."*
> - Johann Wolfgang von Goethe

Warning: Don't Expect this Great Journey to be Easy

Perhaps I have made discovering and living your life-purpose sound a touch too easy. Perhaps I have created the impression that once you know your life-purpose, your problems and challenges will magically vanish.

If you are a dreamer like me, you would like to believe that once you know your life-purpose everything will fall into place, the phone will ring non-stop with people wanting to become clients, with clients wanting you coach them, consult with them, with a dozen opportunities each day, so goes the daydream.

For some of you, discovering your life-purpose may be just the beginning of a much longer journey. According to a bio-documentary about Elijah Harper, the first native person elected to the House of Representatives in Ottawa and the only person who said "No" to the Meech Lake Accord, he got into politics because he wanted to understand non-Indigenous people and how they thought.

For Harper, his election victory was just the beginning of many tall challenges ahead. Every well-known and unknown person with a purpose has faced hurdles, tests, opposition, and challenges. So will you.

You might be wondering why you should bother with all this effort if you're going to face even more difficulties realizing your life-purpose.

Consider the following fact: difficulty spares no one. Consider also the following question: will you face difficulty if you meander and loiter without ever daring to pursue your life-purpose? Of course, you will! If you are going to face difficulty either way, you might as well face it for a worthwhile reward.

When you know and manifest your life-purpose, you will master yourself and your abilities. You will then direct your life instead of being directed by it. Your central aim will be known to you and to those who see your life unfold. Your many victories will be entries on a life-long chain of success, kept alive by your purpose and your positive momentum.

Knowing and living your life-purpose will put you in touch with others on the same path, so to speak, who share the same passion for turning their goals into reality.

Your life-purpose is central to who you are. It is the essence of who you are. It defines what you care about, the difference you want to make. It is your soul's calling.

Through this magnificent process of self-discovery, you will undoubtedly grow and evolve like the man in Chapter 4, like Abel Bosum, Ryan Herjlac, Anne, Lillian, Elijah Harper, and countless others.

On days you feel challenged, hold Saint Theresa's Prayer in mind:

> "May there be peace within today. May you trust God that you are exactly where you are meant to be. May you not forget the infinite possibilities that are born of faith. May you use those gifts that you have received, and pass on the love that has been given to you. May you be content knowing you are a child of God. Let this presence settle into your bones, and allow your soul the freedom to sing, dance, praise and love. It is there for each and every one of us".

Application Exercise: What are Your Next Steps?

Consider action steps you can take right away. Also begin outlining your long-term plan, which you will refine based on experience and feedback from your action steps.

Getting Started

- How can you live fully to be the person you decided to be?
- What can you do about an area that created pain for you in the past? What support or action groups already exist that you can join?
- Whom do you need to meet? Whom do you already know that might have a connection to this person?
- How can you build alliances with the persons you need to meet?
- Where and how can you use your talents and abilities to make a difference?
- Who shares your passion for making a positive difference? How can you build alliances with them?
- What individuals and groups can you speak with about your passion?

Long Term

Remember the Law of Visualization. The world around you is an 'out-picturing' of the world within you.

The images you consistently focus on affect your feelings, your thoughts, and your actions. Whatever you visualize persistently and precisely will eventually materialize in your life. Keep that in mind as you read the points below.

- What is your vision for what you would like to achieve in three to five to ten years?
- Describe it in words, draw it, or find images to create a vision board.
- What actions do you need to take to turn your vision into your reality? By when? Be precise.

EVERY MOMENT IS A FRESH BEGINNING
Start off knowing that nothing can stop you!

Epilogue

The end of one thing is the beginning of something else.
- Author Unknown

My hope is that this book has inspired you to claim your life purpose.

Perhaps, you had a general sense of your life purpose. Using the 5 golden and powerful P Keys, you have gained deeper clarity about your purpose.

If you are not yet living it, now is the time to start and to accelerate it.

A good friend offered this advice from her career experience. Realizing she was not yet in her ideal job, she asked her boss for additional responsibilities to do more of the activities in line with her purpose. She also took some courses to prepare herself for expanded ways to live her life purpose. By being proactive, she was able to live more purposely.

At the end of your life journey, I hope you can say to yourself *"Well done,"* knowing in your heart you have realized what you came here to do and made the difference that is important to you.

"Until one is committed, there is hesitancy, the chance to draw back, always ineffectiveness.

Concerning all acts of initiative and creation, there is one elementary truth the ignorance of which kills countless ideas and splendid plans: That the moment one definitely commits oneself, then providence moves too.

All sorts of things occur to help one that would never otherwise, have occurred. A whole stream of events issue

From the decision, raising in one's favour all manner of unforeseen incidents, meetings and material assistance which no man could have dreamed would have come his way.

> *Whatever you can do or dream you can, begin it. Boldness*
> *has genius, power and magic in it. Begin it now."*
> - William Hutchison Murray

Answer Key: What Is My Purpose?

Individual	Purpose
1. Terry Fox	b. Raised money for the fight against cancer
2. Mother Teresa	a. Showed mercy and compassion to the dying
3. President John F. Kennedy	e. Put a man on the moon
4. Charles Lindberg	h. Be the first person to fly across the Atlantic Ocean
5. Marie Currie	g. Scientist who discovered radium
6. Alexander Graham Bell	c. Built a device for communicating long distances
7. Martin Luther King	f. Achieved equality for all people
8. Nelson Mandela	d. Ended Apartheid
9. Mahatma Gandhi	h. Freed the Indian people from British rule through nonviolent resistance
10. Rosa Parks	g. Civil rights leader – refused to give up her seat for a white man and to go to the back of the bus

Examples: Purpose Statements

I have become a 'Purpose Scout' for discovering people's amazing purposes:

Matthew Coon Come: Defend Aboriginal rights and build the Cree Nation

Ann Talbot: Inspire children to learn and know their magnificence.

Lucy Jeffrey: Help entrepreneurs succeed beyond what they dreamed possible.

Kevin Sandy: Empower and inspire people to live their lives fully.

Dawn T, Maracle: Educate Indigenous people about their history and culture to embrace its magnificence.

Martin Anderson-Clutz: Develop creative solutions for complex technical problems.

Karen Sanche: Encouraging others to live a healthy life.

Agnes Lamers: Help people live healthy, pain free lives.

Shannon Smith: Assist individuals to go from ordinary to unforgettable.

Bill Bishop: Teach people how build a virtual business for the new reality.

Susan Anderson: Transform ordinary writing into clear, powerful and meaningful messages.

Lesley Andrew: Help people discover their voices in every way.

Terry Schmidt: Help smart people transform their business and personal lives by sharing the *Strategic Superpowers*

Jude Thomas: Create, bake to bring joy to people through traditional baking reimagined with love.

Steven Anderson: See God's Kingdom on Earth, see people free, healed and healthy, living abundantly, and without fear.

Agnes Binagwaho: Empower women to revolutionize Rwanda* See below:

file:///Users/marceleneanderson/Desktop/Purpose%20Project/5%20Minute%20Guide%20/Agnes%20Binagwaho:%20How%20women%20are%20revolutionizing%20Rwanda%20%7C%20TED%20Talk.html

After you have developed your purpose statement, send me yours to add the Purpose Club: discoveringyourlifepurpose@gmail.com

References

Bob Kitiell. En-Lighten Up—Enhance Your Mind. Enhance Your Human Connections. Enhance Your Life. 2018. Indigo River Publishing. Pensacola, Florida.

Brian Tracy, Great Little Book on Universal Laws of Success. 1996, Successories Publishing, Lombard, Il.

Jack Canfield, The Success Principles, How to Get from Where You Are to Where You Want to Be. 2005, HarperCollins Publishers, New York, NY.

Mathew Fox, The Reinvention of Work – A New Vision of Livelihood for Our Time, 1994. HarperCollins Publishers, New York, NY.

Richard J. Leider, The Power of Purpose, First Edition, Berrett-Koehler Publishers Inc., 1984. San Francisco.

Viktor Frankl Man's Search for Meaning, A Washington Square Publication of POCKET Books, 1985, New York, NY.

About The Author

Marcelene Anderson, MA, CMC

Marcelene Anderson, founder and CEO of Raven Strategic Solutions, is passionate about helping people to know and realize their life purpose. She is a speaker, facilitator of workshops in guiding people in discovering their life purpose, and creating a plan to live their purpose as well as providing one-on-one and group coaching. On an organizational level, she assists organizational leaders and teams to focus their future direction and develop aligned organizations that achieve results. She also develops the human capacity of organizations.

Marcelene has worked with organizations of all types and sizes, including Fortune 500, First Nations (as referred to in Canada) and Indigenous organizations over a 30-year period. Marcelene has worked with senior corporate management, Chiefs and councils, managers and staff in the following areas: governance planning, strategy, and staff development. She has worked in the following sectors: economic development, financial, marketing and sales, technology, pharmaceutical, transportation, communication, health care, social services, and educational organizations.

Marcelene is a former partner of the Haines Centre for Strategic Management and was a Principal and Senior Management Consultant with KPMG, where she worked extensively with the Grand Council of the Crees (Cree Nation) to implement the James Bay Northern Quebec Agreement.

She is a Certified Management Consultant (CMC), the highest professional standard in management consulting, recognized internationally. As well, she has a Gold Level Certificate in Strategic Management from the Haines Strategic Management Centre. She has provided Change Management and Training Services to a wide range of corporate and public organizations. Over a ten-year period Marcelene worked with community leaders on a voluntary basis across the United States and internationally, to develop and implement methodologies to bring about the transformation of communities.

She has a Masters of Human Systems Intervention from Concordia University in Montreal, Quebec and a Bachelor of Sociology and Psychology Degree from Minnesota State University, Mankato, Minnesota. She also obtained a certificate from McGill University for successfully completing the Executive Development Program. Marcelene is a member of the Canadian Association of Management Consultants.

She is a board of Directors of Ecologos, a non-profit board, dedicated to advocating for protection and sacredness of water and the enviroment.

In addition, she is a member of the New Management Network, a peer group of senior consultants who operate as a virtual organization. She is a member of the Native Canadian Centre of Toronto and a past member of the Canadian Council for Aboriginal Business (CCAB).

Getting in Touch with the Author

For more information about how Marcelene can help you or your organization, please visit www.ravenstrategic.com.

There you will find information about:

- Our Strategic Planning and Implementation process to achieve extraordinary results
- Change management services to realize transformation.

- Services to build and sustain a high-performance organization.
- Programs for developing human capacity, in order to increase performance and productivity.

To connect with Marcelene, send an email to info@ravenstrategic.com and we will get back to you within a day.

Marcelene consults with and speaks to groups throughout North America on developing and successfully implementing strategic plans to transform their nations, communities and organizations as well as facilitating programs to develop human capacity. In addition, she leads in house strategic planning and execution seminars.

Other Books by the Author

For several centuries, Indigenous people in Canada and other parts of the world have had others make decisions for them. The time has come for Indigenous people to once again make decisions for themselves and their future, which is their inherent right.

Taking control requires having a plan for the future. Without a plan, Indigenous people are severely disadvantaged and are likely to have their future dictated by those who assume they have the right to make decisions for them.

The planning process outlined in this book will help you and others tap into your wisdom as well as organize them into a comprehensive, multi-year plan to create the future you want. In developing and implementing your plan, you will discover your ability to make a difference and that you have all you need to realize your desired futures. *Determine Your Future or Someone Else Will* provides insights and practical tools for leaders and organizations that want to chart their own future.

Further Study To Discover Your Life Purpose

In addition to using this book for self-study and reflection, you may get greater value by forming a study group and/or holding *5 Golden Keys to Discovering Your Life Purpose* workshops.

Option 1: Study Group – Hold 7 Study Sessions (approximately 2.5 hours in length)

Week One

1. Introduction – The 5 Powerful Keys To Unlocking Your Life Purpose (to be read in advance)

2. Key 1: People – Choosing Whom You Want to Be and What You Care about

Week Two

3. Key 2: Pain – Transforming Pain, Turning Scars into Stars

Week Three

4. Key 3: Proven Skills and Abilities – Using Your Special Blend of Skills and Abilities to Make a Difference

Week Four

5. Key 4: Passion – Living Your Passion
6. Key 5: Putting It All Together – Creating Your Purpose Master Key

Week Five
7. Choosing Empowering Beliefs

Week Six
8. Accelerating Living Your Purpose

Week Seven (3 weeks later)
9. Dealing with Failure

Week Eight
Progress check up

Option 2: Study Group - Hold 2 Study Sessions (approximately 3.5-4 hours in length)

- Session 1 – Chapters 1-5
- Session 2 – Chapters 6-9

Option 3: Facilitated 1 Day – Discovering Your Life Purpose Workshop

Additional Services

Creating Your Personal Future
Develop a vision for your life congruent with your purpose, set goals and create a personal plan to achieve them.

Strategic and Operational Planning for Organizations
Focus your direction for the future, the results that you want to achieve, and develop operational plans to realize them.

Implementation Support
Put in place a systematic implementation process, to consistently achieve results over time.

Align Employee Purpose with Organizational Purpose
Employees whose purpose is aligned with that of the organization see their work as an opportunity to achieve their personal purpose. They are engaged and produce higher levels of results.

Building High Performance Organizations

Performance Management Process Redesign and Implementation
Establish clear expectations, give feedback regularly, review and monitor performance to improve and sustain high performance

Talent Management and Succession Planning
Reduce turnover and costs of replacing talent, and increase retention of organizational talent.

Capacity Building Programs
Enhance individual and team performance for current and future roles through:

- Coaching for Performance
- Customer Service Skills for Front Line Employees
- Goal-setting and Action Planning
- Governance Training for Boards and Councils
- Interpersonal Communication Skills
- Holding Effective Meetings
- Leadership Development

- Leading Workplace Change for Managers
- Performance Management
- Strategic Planning and Implementation
- Surviving Organizational Change for Employees

Have you been wondering why you are here? What your purpose is? These are questions worthy of your time.

Although you can't do a Google search for your life purpose, the tried, tested and true way to find answers is to ask the right questions, and then discover the answers within. Purpose is fundamental to life. This is a practical book, which will help you answer the 5 Golden Powerful Key questions to unlock your life purpose and how to live life fully.

The book will help you to:

- Affirm who you truly are
- Recognize your proven skills to make a difference
- Turn the pain you have experienced in life to help others
- Focus your passion to live an extraordinary life
- Claim your life purpose, what gives your life meaning
- Gain your Master Key to living fully with Focus, Meaning and Passion

About the Author

Marcelene Anderson is a strategy consultant who works with organizations and their employees to focus their purpose and develop plans to realize it.

For employees to be fully engaged in their work and work place, it is essential that their individual purpose is aligned with the purpose of the organization.

Based on her experience of working with organizations and groups, this book will help you discover the answers within yourself.

"There is no greater gift you can give or receive than to honour your calling. It's why you were born and become most truly alive."
Oprah Winfrey

Is your purpose or time on earth finished? If you are alive, it is not. Seize the opportunity now to unlock and live your life purpose. Embracing your life purpose will help you to soar in life, like a raven.

Printed in the United States
by Baker & Taylor Publisher Services